ASMI

Fatima Hasan

BookLeaf Publishing

Presentation by *BookLeaf Publishing*

Web: www.bookleafpub.com

E-mail: info@bookleafpub.com

ISBN: 978-93-95755-30-6

First edition 2022

*I dedicate this book to my loving children,Hadi
and Zainab.*

ACKNOWLEDGEMENT

I would like to acknowledge my family. A heartfelt thank you to my mother and father for instilling confidence in me to follow my dreams. A big thank you to my two brothers for being there for me, always. And massive gratitude to my husband, who has supported me in all my endeavors.

ASMI

Though she has a lot of names,
I lovingly call her "ASMI",
She is always dressed in spotless white
And strangely, looks a lot like me.

She is my best friend, my confidante.
Has been with me since times immemorial
I still cannot believe how she survives this world
An innocent gold-hearted simple girl.

For her, every hue is black and white
And keeps telling me the wrong and right
Sometimes I listen to her gentle voice
And at other times, I become all deaf.

One thing which I can never understand is,
Why do I feel so angelic when I listen to her?
Complete with a halo around my head,
And why so demonic, a sinner when I don't!

However hard i try, whatever I do to hide,
She always knows the truth bare and white,
I feel like I am an open book to her,
She is my own little replica of God in disguise.

Each one of us has an "Asmi".

Some call it the inner voice
Others call it the subconscious
Asmi is a Sanskrit word meaning "I AM ".

She is the siamese twin I never had.
Within me, with me, Asmi will always lie,
For she, Asmi is the purest part of me.
Untouched by the big, bad world, she is my
SOUL.

SHE UNLIKE ME

I am standing before a mirror,
Reflecting me, a girl, a woman.
I feel blessed and lucky,
For the world has been my oyster.

Turning the mirror upside down,
I see a girl like me, but so unlike me.
I am falling into the abyss of reality
Beyond the neon lights of my urban existence.

Killed while still in her mother's womb.
A curse, an uncurable disease she became,
She unlike me, could never breathe free
Her first breath throttled to become her last.

Poverty and hunger became an inseparable part
of her,
A pain to bear herself on those malnourished
legs,
She unlike me, was frail of body, weak of mind.
A crippled limping frame, a neglected child.

Unlettered, uneducated, and illiterate,
Ignorance became her only companion
She unlike me, never went to school

And never tasted the fruits of education

Married at an early age, a burden eased.
Thrown into the throes of child marriage.
She unlike me, never had any childhood
A flower that never blossomed crushed forever!

A child-woman homebound forever
Multiple miscarriages and premature deliveries
She unlike me, bore insults on her womb
A blessing of God sadly transformed into a curse

In the land of dowry, where money rules the
roost.
For her family, she is a burden, a heavy price to
pay.
She unlike me, was burnt to ashes.
The greed of her in-laws spelled her doom.

She was just like me, but so unfortunate,
Entitled to a bright, fulfilling, and promising
future,
SHE UNLIKE ME was a victim of
circumstances
Perhaps it is still a stigma, a sin to be born a girl!

ON KILLING A
DAUGHTER

She sits there alone,
Her heart too heavy to say anything,
Her soul too aggrieved
Eyes welling up with tears,
Like a dead person in a living body

Because she has killed someone,
And tore a part of her flesh.
 A promising flower, yet to blossom
The world deprived of a unique fragrance
This unborn girl could have been so much,
The light of her life,
The peace of the heart,
The apple of everyone's eyes,
Her mother's own reflection,
A lonely soul's satisfaction,
She could have cried with her, laughed with her,
Whose chattering would have filled the house,
Whose brilliance in everything could be seen by
and all.
Who would have one day wed and said goodbye
That would have been the time to bid farewell,
Not this time to say goodbye to a daughter in her
mother's womb.

FEARLESS NIRBHAYA

Battered and bruised,
Shaken to her core
As her body lay violated.
She became an inspiration,the fearless Nirbhaya

Her body lay trampled and tortured,
Stripped off of her vanity
A young girl bleeding to her death
She made a nation lose sanity.

Horrors of horrors struck her,
Severest of crimes inflicted,
A million deaths in a single life
She made our hearts weep.

Stifled, muffled cries stuck in her throat
That fateful night when terror struck
When she was butchered and butchered.
She put collective memory in havoc.

Imagine her plight,her endless agony
When they ripped out her soul
Unseen,unheard,unimaginable before
She,a fighter,till her last breath!

That night when she took the wrong bus
Who knew it would be the end
She ignited a hidden anger
A burning desire to make amend

She shook the roots of humanity,
Questioned the very existence of it.
Her death gave birth to a revolution
The fires of reform she lit!

In the land of Goddesses,
Where Women are worshipped
She shocked us into dark realities
Truth stared us in face, all falsetto ripped

She was just like me and you,
But her death was one in a million,
A young, promising life to a horrific end.
She made India stand in unison.

Dark-ist

Why does the mind fear?
And my delicate heart quivered
Even a sudden hope of happiness
Fills me with an unimaginable distress

When the dar clouds part ways
To give a glimpse of golden rays
I wait for the darkness to envelope it
And engulf the sunrays bit by bit

Some say, it's a glass half empty
For others, its a glass half full
I know it sounds totally cynical
I see the glass sans water, all nil

Why this deep-rooted war with joy?
Where happiness is not even a short-lived
bubble
Cannot even call me a pessimist
Only a hopeless "Dark-ist" in trouble.

When the mind refuses to go into a happy zone
All it knows is how to feed into despair
Hopelessness and apathy become a part of life,
All i need is everyone's silent prayer.

The road less travelled

It was a long, arduous journey.
Full of agonizing twists and turns
With major obstacles blocking my way.
Still, I took the road less traveled.

They shook their head in disbelief
With nary a doubt in their heads
That I had doom spelled all over me
Still, I took the road less traveled.

My body said no, my legs trembled
Only my instinct guided me
My mind felt like a supreme lord
Still, I took the road less traveled

It was me, and only me.
Who paved the way for them
The cynics and hypocrites who later agreed,
That is why i took the road less travelled.

Survival of the fittest

The world is a concrete jungle
And it is all cut-throat out there
The rats are all running their race
Success, is the only mantra, in their lair.

Using everyone as a ladder,
Climb onto the top and topple you.
Stand right on top of your head,
All they want is an edge over you.

Darwin clued in "Survival of the fittest"
When the frail become the giants
Or perish totally without a trace,
From prey to predator, from friend to fiend!

The Rickshaw-wallah

The shimmering light, charcoal black road
Sweltering un, parched, and merciless
Skeleton of a man pulling a rickshaw
In his sweat, his shirt is drenched!

His stick-thin legs paddling with strain
He looks so old, though, he is young
Getting a dime of money of what he actually
deserves
To him, apathy and poverty clung

Sans dreams and sans hopes,
Of a better and fulfilling future
Carrying loads of people on his back, like a
mule
The rickshaw-wallah humbles one and all!

What is love?

They ask me- What is love?
And I shrug, I haven't a clue.
Maybe it is really undefined.
To make you feel good out of the blue.

Or rather an over-used word
To cover a plethora of emotions
Just society's way to give a name,
To lust, care, affection, and devotion.

For me,it is a shallow sea,
Once you get inside it
It may seem larger and larger
But, once out, it recedes bit by bit.

You may get crazy for love.
At the worst, people kill for this namesake
Or wage ugly wars in its pursuit
But, this is not love, if you are truly awake.

The pursuit of love should be replaced,
By the all-encompassing word of Peace
For it is the one true salvation balm
To a raging storm, like a cool breeze.

Simple pleasures

Simple pleasures of life cannot be,
Measured, they can only be felt.
When one of your hands is held out,
To catch fresh snow, as it melts.

When the wind blows through your ears
whispering in your heart
A sweet little song,
Which stays on for years.

When you see the dew drops,
Falling from leaves
All tears dry up.
Filling you with loads of dreams.

Beautiful birds and tiny butterflies, spreading
their multi-hued, colorful wings
The senses seem to behold the magic of flowers
And eyes see all the varied emotions mingling

That rainbow which you see after the rain
appears to be a twisted happy smile on the sky
drifting blue ethereal clouds
In which the birds fly.

It rained that day

I was walking all alone on a road
No one in front, not one soul behind
Just me, my loneliness, and the rain
Only water drops everywhere I could find.

Sounds of thunders, lightning agony everywhere
dark black clouds hovering on my head
Everything is covered with a melancholy
And I don't know what lead me, what lay ahead.

Why was nature echoing my feelings?
Like somehow it knew my heart's pain
My teardrops and raindrops were now all one
No one could see me cry in the rain.

The Mirage

Walking through an endless desert
Searching for that ever-elusive mirage
I did not know where it was or
What it was, but I continued my voyage

I saw an oasis at a distance
Full of gold and precious gems
Running breathlessly towards it,greedy-eyed
My mind had lost all rhythm and sense

But to my horror, it was nothing
Only priceless glittering sand
Suddenly, I was bathed in divine light
Radiating a light so pure, my eyes could not
stand.

Had I entered a new world?
Far away from that desert
A comfortable numbness had enveloped me
Heart,soul,body now all in dirt

All throughout my life,i ran after money
Which was nothing but sand,i realised
that illusion,that mirage was my life
Which had faded, and I had died and I had died.

The Light

It is a pitch dark moonless night
An eerie silence, so melancholically blanketing
me
Not a single soul anywhere in sight
I walk alone, all alone on this unknown road

As though I am blindfolded and gagged,
I wander aimlessly like a haggard beggar
Trying to seek answers to impossible questions,
my spirits sagged
My tears blind my eyes and pain pierces my
heart.

This long long night never seems to end.
I had stopped believing "HIM", the almighty
Lord.
My soul is broken into million pieces,it cannot
be mend
Stuck in the claws of perdition, I have been
cured.

Lo! Behold! I see a flicker of light, so pure and
white.
To my battered self, it seems like a mirage

Suddenly my mirage becomes a miraculous
sight
The first rays of hope penetrate my agony-filled
heart.

I am bathed in divine light, so serene and pure
Yes! He finally answered my prayers
My black nights transform into a starry sky
The faith in you, my lord, burns in me bright.

My first snowfall

I lay asleep in my snug blanket
Lost in a warm and lovely sleep
Spinning up a thousand splendid dreams
My slumber was comforting and deep

Suddenly, I heard some animated chatter
My friends were all around me, giggling and
tittering
I slowly opened my eyes to a fresh morning
The view from the window was
oh-so-fascinating

Snowflakes were falling like dew drops
It was a serenely blissful sight,
As if God was sending showers of blessings,
Transforming the mundane to illuminating
bright

Together, we all made a snowman
Complete with a pudgy nose and beady eyes
Our snowballing sessions and trysts with the
camera
Made it the best morning of my life.

Despite the cold, our hearts felt the warmth

Draping her child with a white blanket
Mother nature was at her best
"Unforgettable",my first snowfall was heaven on
earth.

Flight of existence

A little egg cracked, opening out
And tiny eyes peeped out of them
It was her world, without a doubt
A "jailed existence" is all she thought.

Her initial glee was replaced by agony
Though she was fed and cared for,
Because her life was itself an irony
Her wings were unflustered and lifeless

Day and night, she dreamt of flying
Of spreading her wings up and high
Her false hopes, promises lying
Confined indoors, she had never seen a flight.

She hoped she prayed, she dreamt
Of this single threadbare of existence
Days and nights, months and years swept
One fine day, the door was left ajar

She saw a little bird, like herself
Hop out of her nest and take a flight
She stayed transfixed, her wings electrified
She flew and she flew, her future finally bright.

Amen!

If wishes had wings,
If dreams turned into reality
If mirages were indeed true,
And if I could fly!

I would have been a free bird
Soaring high up in the skies
Fluttering my beautiful wings
Up above and so high!

In a place full of calm and peace
My mind at its blissful best
I would frolic around like a bubble
And give all the worries a long rest

My mind which was previously unkempt
Now turned into a beautiful garden
All the pessimism spilling out of me,
Positivity coming true like an "Amen"

It seems like a utopian land
Where life is beyond paradise
Surreal, magical and so untrue
Beyond the realms of human existence.

With pain, comes prayer

I knelt and bowed down in front of Him
He was standing all majestic and tall
Murmuring a faint prayer on my lips,
With my eyes closed, I saw Him in his full glory.

His rays of magnificence reached out
The Lord of Lords shone brightly
My eyes kept shut, unable to open at all
Quivering with his all-encompassing light

I knew i had forgotten all about Him
Daring to call myself an "atheist"
But still he stood before me,
Like a wake-up call,He came!

To wake me up from my long slumber,
To fill hope in my starved soul
To brim my heart up with peace
To replace my pain with pleasure

He knew all my agonies and the deep hurt
Was never a stranger to my whole being
Nothing in the world was a balm,
He was all i sought and yearned

Nobody ever had understood me
For i was beyond the textbook definitions
But He,He knew it all
Understood all my trials and tribulations

I had no one except Him
and having Him,meant the world to me.
Turning my curse into a blessing,
He had transformed my pain to prayer.

The Cemetry

On my way to work today,
I saw a beautiful cemetery!
Lush green and serene
In the hustle and bustle of the busy city
It was an island of quiet
In a place of people centricity
Those plaques meant people long gone
Walking on similar pathways with their worries
With similar commutes to their workplaces
We do not know their life stories
All that is left is their loved ones
And a plethora of memories!
Living or dead!! We all go the same six feet
under.
Make it a memorable life to die with dignity!!

Tooth fairy

I saw her as she walked into the clinic
A beautiful little girl with anxious eyes
With a toothache, in pain, and sick
Clutching her father's fingers

I was called by the in-charge-teacher,
And he said," Case allotted to you"!
I was equally nervous as her
That day was my first day at the clinic, a place
new

The nervousness slowly melted away
When I held her little hands
Through her pain, I had to make my way
As if a tooth fairy had granted me a magic wand

To calm her, I had to silence my fears
And fight against the cloud of insecurity
"Your toothache will vanish, my dear"!
As I said this to her, she became my
responsibility.

Sometime later, I was content and happy
A thankful smile lit up her face, her anxiety
replaced by glee.

"Every tooth has a soul attached to it,
This quote became all truthful to me.

The medical student

"Why do you want to be a doctor"?
They asked me in a medical school interview
And I felt my heart tugging at my head,
For I saw my decade-long struggle, in a
flashback, a single view.

"Were you not a dentist in India?"
Then why med school in Australia, as a
mature-aged student
You are also a mum of two young children
Surely, you must have a busy household!", they
comment.

"Why do you want to study again?"
Could a nine-to-five job suffice for you?
Take care of your children now,
And maybe have some hobbies, one or two!

Such a rigorous timetable and so much study
Busy mothers like you, would not survive
How would you do justice to med school?
There are other careers, that pay dozen a dime.

I laugh at all these questions and I say,
"Med school is my one true passion,

And I feel that medicine is my first child.
It needs nurturing and a lovelike devotion.

The human body is an amazing creation,
Of the one above, the almighty Lord.
Its wonders never cease to amaze me,
The never-ending curiosity, how it unfolds!

I am happy to burn the midnight oil,
And I am pleased to be on this exciting journey
Because I have never been so content,
With any other decision in my life.

I faced failures after failures,
And finally, I got into med school on merit,
I count each day as a blessing
And give everyone their due credit.

I love listening to my patients' stories
And think deeply and reflect on human suffering
One day, I aspire to be someone's giver of hope
Being a doctor touches the deepest chords of our
being.

Lord Cunningham

Throwing the caution to the winds
Here comes Lord Cunningham
His name is his prized possession
Borne out of a century of bloodlust

The stakes are onto his head,
The army galloping to kill him
Hordes of naked swords around,
The glint of metal, un merciful!

The king of the land was once his lord
For whom Cunningham waged battles
Now the king said, "Off with his head"!
In his regal, punishing baritone.

The king's only son, a young prince
Was lying on his deathbed
The healers exhausted all their potions
Till the witches came, was the folklore.

They cackled, "Sacrifice the blood of a
braveheart"!
One whose life was full of conquests
At the burning pyre of his body
The prince will regain good health.

All this voodoo was a necessity,
To cure the king's only son
An heir to the throne
A worthy sacrifice to be made.

So, the king chose Lord Cunningham,
To sacrifice his life at the prince's deathbed
The kingdom cried, the skies wept
For Cunningham was a noble man

Cunningham being a loyal soul
The love for motherland, flowed in his veins
And if all they wanted was his life
He would gladly give his own

The nights grew darker,
The air was treacherous and still
The witches gathered around
In a cocktail of blood and fire

The prince lay shrouded in a garment
His body covered head to toe,
What lay beneath that garment,
Lord Cunnigham never knew

It was a ploy to get him killed,
For Cunningham was loved by all
The King grew jealous of him day and night

And feared for his precious crown

Maybe the wind caught the scent of betrayal
For it blew and blew, uncovering the garment
Beneath it was a boy, not the prince at all
Lo ! Behold! it was a treacherous predicament

Seize him! Off with his head, roared the king!
I want to see him die now! Enough with the
dramatics
Off with all his ideas to seize my kingdom,
Kill him, behead him, before any more tricks!

And so, Cunningham galloped on his horse,
Fighting with a seething rage in him
And killed all the king's henchmen
With his faithful sword

"O great King, I loved and respected you, with
nary a doubt.
I was ready to sacrifice my life, and mark my
word.
To save the prince, my death would suffice.
But you plotted to kill me, my Lord!

"I renounce your kingdom, I renounce your land
I renounce the bloodlust on my hands!", said he
reaching the woods

"Never will I return back to your kingdom, Tis'
all over!
I will not seek revenge or kill you, O king! No
more blood!"

www.ingramcontent.com/pod-product-compliance
Lightning Source LLC
Chambersburg PA
CBHW061319140726
47998CB00006B/2471